The Seal of the

Living God

Revelation 7:2

By Tom Coyle

"Do not harm the land or the sea or the trees until we
put a seal on the forehead of the servants of our God."
Revelation 7:3

i

Acknowledgement

"To my amazing wife, Georgia Roy, this book wouldn't have been possible without your unwavering support and encouragement. Your love, patience, and belief in me have been my rock, and I'm forever grateful. Thank you for being my partner in every sense of the word. I love you more than words can express."

Introduction

There was no AI used in the production of this book. All the words in this book are my own unless otherwise noted, and even the designs were made by me using publisher and PowerPoint.

This Book is not meant for everyone. If you love living a lie this book will mean nothing to you. If you are an unbeliever this book might open your eyes to the truth. If you are rigid in your religious beliefs because it's what you have done your whole life, this book might open your eyes to the truth. If you left your religion or church because of hypocrisy you will likely find your place in the words of this book. If you are a true child of God this book may give you a renewed hope in your salvation. And if you are just looking for truth, welcome to the family. The time is short; you need to choose sides now.

"Come now, and let us reason together, saith the Lord: though your sins be as scarlet, they shall be white as snow; though they be red like crimson, they shall be as wool." Isaiah 1:18 KJV

I am not a Bible Scholar, neither were most of the disciples. What I can say is that I have a long relationship with God through His Word and He has taught me and has opened my eyes to amazing things, but the most amazing thing is that I have gotten to know God on a very personal level. He is indeed my very best friend.

For Forty years I have read the Bible Daily, I have

read the Bible front to back over 78 times along with a plethora of other books and manuscripts like Eusebius, Josephus, and the Dead Sea Scrolls. I listened to sermons given by true believers whose love of God came shining through.

And I prayed every day for 40 years that the Lord would open my eyes to His Word. In that time I have built a friendship with the
Lord that will last an eternity, and I would never intentionally lie about my friend or His Word.

This book will not likely be endorsed by any religion, nor do I want it to be endorsed by any established religion. But I really would appreciate an endorsement from those of you who love the Word as much as I do, by giving this book to someone else (after you have read it) who just might see the value in it.

May the Lord of all and the giver of all good, bless you mightily!

Front cover image by: Tom Coyle
Book design by: Tom Coyle
Contact: thesealofthelivinggod@proton.me

Table of Contents

ix

x

Chapter 1

The Heart of the Matter

Truth: from the Old English trEowth meaning fidelity to the facts or subject matter. It has the connotation of a commitment as intense as a marriage vow. In other words, truth has to be completely dedicated to the facts with no external influences.

At the heart of every matter is the truth of that matter. Many throughout history have tried to describe truth; the most popular descriptions however, have come from philosophers like Rene Descartes, David Hume, and Immanuel Kant. These are scholarly thinkers who try to define truth as a concept or perception that may or may not be subjective. Epistemology is the study of how knowledge is acquired. There are two trains of thought in this discipline; Empiricism and Rationalism are how philosophers explain the process of gaining knowledge.

Empiricism states that all knowledge comes from prior experiences, and that is the only way knowledge can be acquired. Rationalism says that knowledge can come from our ability to rationalize as well as through our experiences. The reality is that Rationalism can only use known or presumably known facts on which to base a rationale and those known facts had to have come from previous knowledge. If that previous knowledge is faulty, our Rationalism will be faulty as well. Rationalization is the application of known or presumed facts and does not lead to new facts, rather it points to unanswered questions to which we seek an experience or experimentation, if you will, to try and answer those questions. It is simply our interpretation of what those facts are and how we choose to apply them. The problem is that our interpretation is often a result of faulty facts or a bias towards a desired outcome.

Few men in history had the reasoning power of Thomas Edison yet it took him over 1000 tries to come up with a light bulb. Each try produced results (or facts if you will) that lead to further reasoning, further rationalization, and further attempts. In other words, Edison learned from his mistakes. He did not rationalize the light bulb into existence, rather he learned from his mistakes until the experience led him to the right conclusion. How did he know it was the right conclusion? Because when he sent electricity through the wires, *a light came on.* I am sure that more than once during the trial and error process he thought that he had the right formula. When tested however, he was convinced he was wrong and plotted another course.

Rationalization does not produce knowledge, it only leads us to seek additional knowledge through experimentation of what we already know.

Reasoning and rationalization are two very different things. These two words have been frequently interchanged with each other, and dictionaries even use one word to describe the other.

We must find a clear and concise definition for each of these terms. To save future confusion I will define these two terms as they pertain to this writing.

Reasoning: *the process of interpreting, and judging the validity of the facts to get a clearer understanding of what those facts mean.*

Rationalism: *using known or presumably known facts to discover, promote, conceive or apply a solution to a question or problem.*

Humans are the only creatures on earth with reasoning power and the ability to rationalize. Instinct tells a dog to seek shelter in a rainstorm, but a dog could not use reasoning to understand the problem, nor use rationalization to design and construct a shelter. We humans take this reasoning power and rationalization for granted, and when things are taken for granted they are often misused or abused.

In the movie *Indiana Jones, Raiders of the Lost Ark,* Professor Jones tell his archeology class "archeology is the study of facts, if it is truth you are looking for, you need to sign up for a philosophy course".

The reality is that philosophy is a belief system much like religion is a belief system. So what does philosophy and religion have to do with each other? They are both belief systems based on *questionable* reasoning and rationalization to promote a commonly shared ideology within their select groups. I say *questionable* because in philosophy there are many different camps or schools of thought, and religion has an overabundance of different, doctrines, rituals and practices, all of which can only lead to the conclusion that a bias is prevalent in most, if not all of their reasoning and rationalization.

In both philosophy and religion, assumptions are made that their interpretation of the facts is a genuine reflection of the truth, yet there can only be one truth. A religious person believes in a certain doctrine and a philosopher believes in a certain school of thought within that discipline. Both are based on faith in their power of reasoning and rationalization. That is, their personal interpretation of the facts as they see them. But is truth dependent on our interpretation of the facts?

When things are left to our own bias, we tend to fault in the favor of those biases leaving an impression of righteousness in our thinking, but in reality we have perverted the facts that could and should lead us to the real truth. I say real truth, not because there is a false truth, but because of a false interpretation of the truth, which leads us to accepting a lie as the truth.

Rene Descartes, a well-respected philosopher of modern times and a proponent of rationalism, stated, "I think, and therefore I am." Quite a profound statement and it even sounds reasonable. In truth however, Descartes' statement lacks substance of fact. See, even if Descartes didn't think, he would still exist, much the same as a rock exists. A good philosopher would undoubtedly ask how I could know for a fact that the rock really exists. The answer of course is the evidence. I see it, I feel it, and I know without a doubt that if I pick it up and throw it at a window, the window will break. Furthermore, witnesses to such an action would concur that indeed it was a rock. Philosophers are willing to use any devise they can to prove their theories, except evidence, because evidence might prove them wrong.

The first and foremost criterion for scientific evidence is that it must be capable of being proven wrong as well as being proven right. Therefore any scientific statement must meet this criterion, (i.e. the moon is made of green cheese). This is truly a scientific statement because we have been to the moon and in fact it was not made of green cheese, but of rocks and dust. Thus the statement can and was proven wrong. The statement, the moon is made of rocks and dust is equally scientific because it has been proven right. It is not necessary to prove or disprove a statement for it to be truly scientific, it only needs the possibility of being proven and disproved for it to be scientific.

There is an either-or, true-or-false, right-or-wrong in science, not so in philosophy (they think, and therefore they must be right). Ironically, the term philosophy comes from the Greek word (Philosophia) meaning love of truth. A detail concerning anything is either true or false. If we find that there is some truth and some falseness to a detail, we have more than one detail, and they need to be broken down. Many people find a negative aspect of a statement and throw the whole statement out rather than breaking down the statement into separate parts and only discarding the false parts. The reverse is also true: accepting a statement that is partially true and accepting the falsehood along with it.

Context is another important criterion in finding truth. In the book of Exodus, God, speaking to Moses says,"I am that I am". That being the case, it could be argued that since Descartes says, "I think, and therefore 'I am'," he must be God. Of course this is absurd, the two "*I am*" are not at all connected, but when you're trying to prove a preconceived notion, many tend to stretch the envelope by any means at their disposal. For every detail, there is a truth. Not knowing the truth of that detail, or not even considering that the detail has any impact whatsoever on the truth of that detail, will only changes how we perceive the truth of that detail.

What about things I cannot see or feel, like Mr. Descartes who has been dead for a couple hundred years. I can't see him, that's for sure, nor can I feel him, nor can I throw him through a window. There is however, quite a bit of evidence that supports the fact that indeed Mr. Descartes existed. If there weren't I would not have been compelled to write the last few paragraphs. Even though I cannot see, feel, or throw Mr. Descartes, there does exist compelling, albeit circumstantial evidence that supports as fact that he did exist.

Circumstantial evidence, however, cannot totally be accepted as fact since it only supports the fact in some way and is never conclusive. This is not to say that circumstantial evidence is void of merit. Such evidence must be weighed and the weight applied to the heart of the matter, and to be, as it were, weighted influence towards whichever side it supports.

If the only evidence I had to go on for Mr. Descartes' existence is the fact that he is mentioned in numerous books, then I would have equally as much circumstantial evidence to prove Santa Claus existed. There is quite a difference however, If I asked someone if Mr. Descartes actually existed they would likely say yes, but with Santa, the answer is likely to lose the majority of support to the negative side. Why? Because the preponderance of the circumstantial evidence is clear. That is to say, the evidence is very compelling when we consider whether Mr. Descartes' existed, and not so compelling for dear Old Santa.

Evidence should be evaluated according to the weightiness of the known facts. The fact that there are more pictures floating around of Santa than of Mr.

Descartes does not lend weight to Santa's cause, because we all know that it is a tradition for people to dress up as Santa during the Holidays. Likewise, most pictures of Santa

are obvious caricatures rather than real photo-graphic reproductions. There are no photo-graphic images of Mr. Descartes since he had been dead for over a hundred years before that technology existed. The artist's likenesses of Mr. Descartes however, are obviously intended to be an honest attempt at capturing the true nature of Mr. Descartes rather than a caricature of him.

When more evidence supports an assumption, we tend to have more faith that our hypothesis is correct, and rightly so, but should that be the end of the matter? The preponderance of evidence for Mr. Descartes' existence (i.e. most people believe he existed, there is a grave site with his name on the tombstone, mentioned in numerous writings etc.) strongly point to the possibility of this person's existence, but it is hardly conclusive.

To be conclusive, we would need documented birth or death records and dental records that match the cadaver buried in the tomb. We could also rely on eyewitnesses or a constant chain of evidence from the time Mr. Descartes presumably existed until now. This would lead to an undisputable determination that he in fact existed. The first three are exhausted due to constraint; however, the fourth and final possibility is indeed available for consideration. When reasoned out, (i.e. other people who lived during the time period recognized Mr. Descartes existence through their writing, etc.), we can rationalize *with reservation* that Mr. Descartes actually did exist. We can now use this fact to rationalize further. Should the work attributed to Mr. Descartes be accredited to him?

To my knowledge, all the work accredited to Mr. Descartes is dated back to the time of his presumed existence. If it was dated before Descartes birth or after his death it would indicate that he could not have written these works. Further evidence would indicate that other writers in the same period accredit these works to Mr. Descartes. All the written works of Mr. Descartes (to my knowledge) are about philosophical ideologies, which would further indicate their authenticity. If you found a writing that had Mr. Descartes' name as the author, and the writing was about how to gap a spark plug, it would definitely indicate that the author was not the same Mr. Descartes we are talking about here, for two reasons. One, it was not within the authors expertise, and two, spark plugs were not invented at the time Mr. Descartes existed.

Likewise, if a reputable source at the time of Mr. Descartes' existence disputed that he actually produced that work which is accredited to him; it would throw a shadow of doubt over his authorship of the work. To my knowledge, this is not the case, so through reasoning we can assume, *with reservation that* Mr. Descartes actually existed, and he in fact was the author of those works that are accredited to him. I say with reservation because we have not conclusively proven his existence, but we have eliminated any reasonable doubt through all the available knowledge on the matter. We would consider this trustworthy information simply on the grounds that the likelihood of being misled is infinitesimal.

The process we just went through has not proven that Mr. Descartes actually existed. It only validates our reason to believe that he existed. We have not gained new knowledge through rationalization, all we did was validate, through reasoning, that the knowledge we do have is as trustworthy as we can make it. We do this by looking at all the available facts without prejudice.

Have we proven that knowledge cannot come through rationalization? Absolutely not! But we have questioned the process and discovered that the likelihood of gaining knowledge through rationalization is minuscule to the point that it should not be considered as a valid certainty.

There is an enormous difference between knowledge and truth. Knowledge is just a tool we use to find the truth. I have heard many people refer to different kinds of truth, (i.e. partial truth, absolute truth, prevailing truth etc.). When the fact is, if it is not absolute, it is not truth, and is only our limited understanding of what the truth is. In other words, it is knowledge to be used as a tool to find even more certainty.

Knowledge can be partial and prevailing but in all cases it is never absolute. To be absolute, that knowledge would have to include every detail of every possibility throughout the universe and through all time frames. Why? Because truth is throughout the universe and through all time frames, so who could know how each detail truly affects the other unless all truth were known. We cannot, and so we rely on what knowledge we do have and our reasoning and rationalization power to discover more knowledge in hopes that we can use that knowledge to gain understanding of who and what we are, and to gain understanding of the world and universe we live in.

The world is round, just about everyone over the age of eight knows this. Prior to 1492 only a select few even suspected it to be round. I'd say it is safe to assume that the world was round long before Columbus discovered that fact. Now it is an indisputable fact. Since it is undisputable can we refer to it as a truth? Yes! It is *a* truth, because it has been proven to meet our definition of round. The point is that long before we discovered it was round, it met our definition of being round. Truth is not dependent on us finding it, we are dependent on finding it to gain knowledge.

Does a lie, change the truth in any way? No! It only changes our perception of the truth, and since truth is not dependent on our understanding, we are the only ones who suffer the consequences of a lie. Can anything alter change, destroy, manipulate, or weaken a truth? No! It can only alter, change, destroy, manipulate, or weaken our perception of what the truth is.

If someone asked me to describe the world, and I simply said it is round, would that be a partial truth? No, it would be a whole truth, the world is round. It would however, be a partial answer.

The problem is that any answer short of a complete history, geography, sociology, genealogy, and chronology of everything that took place from the foundation of the world until now, would still be a partial answer even if every fact was a whole truth. To answer every question that completely would be unreasonable, and in most cases a cursory answer that covers a general description will suffice.

There is a problem however, with general descriptions that end up being the basis of a presumed truth. Columbus thought he proved that the world was round only because he thought he had landed in India. The world was round, and he did lead the way, but the fact is that Columbus was not the one to prove it. That distinction goes to the Spanish sailor Ferdinand Magellan.

Columbus acted out of confidence in the knowledge he had concerning the shape of the earth. He trusted the knowledge he had and his reasoning and rationalization power, which, after acting upon, led to the discovery of a significant truth and new knowledge.

Philosophers think of truth as a concept rather than a fact. Columbus did conceptualize the world to be round, but the world was not made round because Columbus had that particular concept. The concept however, was very important to the discoveries that Columbus made because it pointed him in the right direction, while his faith in that concept motivated him to set sail in search of truth. Truth is not a concept, truth is a fact. When we use a fact to lead us into a significant truth, it is usually because we conceptualized that there is more to learn.

If Columbus just conceptualized the truth without actually setting sail, he would never have found the truth. He needed something else to bring his concept into reality. He needed enough motivation to actually push him to act upon his precepts. He was motivated in his heart to find the truth.

Think of our brain as a high-powered rifle, truth as the target, and the scope we look through to see the target as our heart. Our motivation, which comes from the heart, is in direct correlation with the scopes power and its accuracy. The more we want to see the real truth, the more motivation we will have, but if we are looking for an acceptable compromise with the truth, our aim will be off in correlation with our motive. We may miss the truth completely, simply because our motivation was leaning in one direction or the other rather than directly on the truth. If our brain (i.e. knowledge) is a little off we will be aiming at the wrong target and we will end up missing the target as well. But we still need to pull the trigger, so we need a physical being in order to make the shot. We need a finger to pull the trigger, eyes to line up the shot, and a steady hand to hold the gun in place. The character or soul of a person is the relationship between the rifle, the scope, and the body, making it a unit. If any part of the unit is out of place, or off kilter, it will affect the shot.

Now a steady hand is fairly easy to come by when shooting at a benign target, but what if the target is a charging bull. Fear may get in the way of our ability to make the shot. Fear does not help the process; it hinders it, sometimes to our own detriment. We experience some kind of emotion continually, and how it affects our performance is a critical issue when we are searching for truth. As an example, let's go back to Christopher Columbus and his journey. What if he thought the world was round, and was motivated to somehow prove it, but he was just too scared to go on the journey for fear of being shipwrecked or a storm at sea. Christopher Columbus would have been a complete unknown today had he not had the faith in his concept to risk life and limb to prove it right. Faith and emotions will be covered in future chapters, but here it is important to note the correlation they have to finding truth.

I have said little about religion, because I did not want to offend or upset the delicate nature and loyalty that exists in people of faith. It is important however, to examine the validity of the concepts that form that faith in which we put so much trust. Here is the question that needs answered: Is your particular faith or concept of God based on a comprehensive search for truth, or is it based on a preconceived notion of what you want God to be. There is nothing wrong with having a concept, even a wrong concept, when tested, serves as a learning tool as long as we diligently seek the complete unmitigated truth of the matter. Concepts point us in a certain direction but if we never go on the journey we will never know for sure if our understanding of the concept is correct. Concepts need to be tested.

Today people travel the world in all different directions having confidence that they will not fall off the edge of the world. This confidence is shared by everyone on this planet. We don't need to question the fact since it has been proven true. With regard to religion however, there are many different views and opinions and concepts and faiths, which differ to the point of complete opposites in some cases.

Most people on this planet believe that there is one God (mono-theistic) rather than many gods (polytheistic). If indeed that is the case, that there is only one God, how can there be so many different views about whom or what He is. The answer is simple, there are a lot of people who are putting their confidence in a wrong concept.

How do I know this to be true? Because if there is only one God and that one God is based on the God of the Bible which encompasses all Christians, Islamic and Jewish factions, it constitutes about 55 % of the religious population of the world. Then we must be talking about the same God in principal. But is He really the same God. The God that the Jews profess loves Israel, while the God professed by Islam hates Israel. And the God of Christians seems to love everyone. Christians profess Jesus as the Messiah: Jews are still waiting on a Messiah: and Islam looks to Mohammed as a messiah of sorts.

Each major religion is also broken down into numerous sects that further dilute these major religions into a hodgepodge of different mini-religions, each claiming to be the one true religion. In truth, however, there can only be one true religion. We will cover this subject in-depth in a later chapter, but here it is important to know that there are huge differences, and we need to understand how those differences relate to truth.

What about atheism, agnosticism, and apathy, what basis is there for such concepts, and is it based on truth? I have never met an atheist or agnostic who has read the bible front to back, though many of them can quote certain pass-ages on which they base their beliefs (usually out of context) and give the appearance that they know what they are talking about. This is not to say that there are none that have read the bible front to back, only that those I have come in contact with have not. For that matter, of the people I do know, there are very few professing Christians,

Jews, or Islamic people who have read the bible front to back.

Many have grown up in situations where they have seen hypocrisy in certain religions and have rejected the entire religious concept instead of searching for the truth. A concept is nothing more than an opinion: but should an opinion based on preconceived notions and bias carry the same weight as one based on evidence, research, and reasoning. Of course not!

Many people do not believe in a god at all. One such concept is that God was created by man to put restraint on man's activities and keep him from having fun. An appealing concept that too many people have: only one problem with it. If man likes to have fun, which I am sure most people do, then why would man create a

God that would keep him from having fun? And the tip of the iceberg is: why would so many people believe in a God who would keep them from having fun? There just isn't any logic to this concept, but it is a popular one with atheists and agnostics.

When it comes to those who are apathetic towards the existence of God, here is a wake-up call you will suffer damnation even if you think believing in the Living God waste of your time. On the other hand we have Nietzsche who claimed that God was dead. Another of the respected Philosophers of the 19th century, Nietzsche is the father of those who believe that God was a myth created to control and subject man to a form of life contrary to his nature. To Nietzsche the bigger crime was to expect man to be subjected to such a repressive form of existence.

"To speak of right and wrong per se makes no sense at all. No act of violence, rape, exploitation, destruction, is intrinsically unjust, since life itself is violent, rapacious, exploitative, and destructive, and cannot be conceived otherwise."

-Friedrich Nietzsche

Obviously Nietzsche puts very little value in such things as love, compassion, loyalty, mercy, kindness, consideration, trustworthiness and a whole slew of positively motivated human characteristics that encompasses a considerable part of humanity.

The thing is, Nietzsche is not altogether wrong, "life itself is violent, rapacious, exploitative, and destructive," but it doesn't have to be, and it is not always the case. And just because at times it is, that is no justification for humans, who have the ability to discern right from wrong, to choose wrong. The fact that someone like Friedrich Nietzsche is even considered as having a valid viewpoint on the subject is simply astounding. But his teachings will continue to influence as long as people want to hear half-truths. In today's society Friedrich Nietzsche is held in great regard and as a truly enlightened individual, and the fact that he was totally insane at a very early age only lends credibility to his brilliance as far as certain academics are concerned. Tell me, could it be possible that Friedrich Nietzsche was insane long before he was diagnosed?

The most renown of modern day thinkers is Immanuel Kant, the father of agnostics everywhere. He firmly believed that physical matter was just an illusion that we share collectively. In fact, he believed that the only thing that really did exist was that which is in our reasoning power to perceive. Kant believed that reason is the final authority for morality as well. [1]

"Actions of any sort, he believed, must be undertaken from a sense of duty dictated by reason, and no action performed for expediency or solely in obedience to law or custom can be regarded as moral. Kant described two types of commands given by reason: the hypothetical imperative, which dictates a given course of action to reach a specific end, and the categorical imperative, which dictates a course of action that must be followed because of its rightness and necessity. The categorical imperative is the basis of morality and was stated by Kant in these words: "Act as if the maxim of your action were to become through your will a general natural law."

"Kant's ethical ideas are a logical outcome of his belief in the fundamental freedom of the individual as stated in his *Critique of Practical Reason* (1788). This freedom he did not regard as the lawless freedom of anarchy, but rather as the freedom of self-government, the freedom to obey consciously the laws of the universe as revealed by reason. He believed that the welfare of each individual should properly be regarded as an end in itself and that the world was progressing toward an ideal society in which reason would "bind every law giver to make his laws in such a way that they could have sprung from the united will of an entire people, and to regard every subject, in so far as he wishes to be a citizen, on the basis of whether he has conformed to that will." In his treatise *Perpetual Peace* (1795) Kant advocated the establishment of a world federation of republican states." (i.e. one world Government)[1]

In all fairness to Kant, he was not trying to prove that God did not exist like so many of the other philosophers. He was in fact looking to find God within reason. It is a shame he was unable to see that God is so far beyond our capability to reason that faith is the only open door that we have.

---

[1] "Kant, Immanuel," *Microsoft® Encarta® 97 Encyclopedia.* © 1993-1996 Microsoft Corporation. All rights reserved.

So here's the problem, I pick up a rock and throw it through my neighbor's window, (keeping in mind that this is just a collectively shared perception) and *everyone* who witnessed it, will attest to the fact that I broke the window. But if you asked the witnesses about whether it was wrong of me to break my neighbor's window you would get an overabundance of different answers.

So why is it that the physical world is a collectively shared experience, but not so when it comes to "the laws of the universe as revealed by reason"? You can't have it both ways.

When a philosopher denies a physical world he or she then makes everything subjective to his or her own reasoning. To prove or disprove is no longer an option, even for weighted evidence since that is also subjective.

Now it's been 200 years since the death of Mr. Kant and I just don't see that "the world is progressing toward an ideal society in which reason would 'bind every law giver to make his laws in such a way that they could have sprung from the united will of an entire people, and to regard every subject, in so far as he wishes to be a citizen, on the basis of whether he has conformed to that will.'" It's just not happening, and it never will from that type of thinking. Many people today are brain washed to a certain way of subjective thinking, yet it has not made the world a better place by any means.

Let's go back to Thomas Edison for a minute. What if Thomas Edison developed the theory that sending electricity through a wire will create light? And let's say that every known thinker of his day agreed with his theory even though it had never been proven. What if a century had passed and the light bulb still had not been invented, but every known expert on the matter was still proclaiming Thomas Edison's theory correct. It certainly sounds correct and it makes perfect sense but without a working model it would still be a pipe dream. Once you decide to use a carbon filament in a vacuum you will get light, a very important part of the equation.

Yet these philosophers and academics come up with all sorts of good sounding but unproven theories, which a good number of other philosophers and academics back up, with little or no proof. And why do they back them up when the proof is so deceptive? So in academia, if you want someone to corroborate your work, you have to reciprocate by corroborating their work. They know that skeptics will question their own shoddy theories, so the one hand washes the other.

Every lie has a measure of truth in it, so as to validate that lie. Political spin is a good example of lies that are supplemented with the truth. "Fahrenheit 9/11," the Michael Moore film that portrayed the politics surrounding the World Trade Center disaster and the War on Terrorism with such graphic detail, had more spin than any gyroscope could ever hope to achieve. There was a lot of truth in the movie, and in actuality very few out and out lies, though there might have been some, but the main thing is, there was a whole lot of truth that was left out, and it resulted in innuendos that were very misleading, intentionally.

Using truth in support of a lie is as old as Adam and Eve in the garden. What the serpent told Eve was not altogether a complete fabrication. In fact it had more truth than lie, they did gain the consequences of "the knowledge of good and evil", the hard way. And they didn't die physically right away, they just died spiritually. The only thing that made them like God was that they now knew the consequences of "the knowledge of good and evil" which is adversity and joy, mostly I'm afraid, they knew adversity. Joy they already had in the garden, but they took it for granted. But, alas, people are going to believe what they want.

Here is some truth that might add a little weight to it however: Michael Moore is a Hollywood producer, not a news source. Michael Moore promotes Michael Moore's agenda and gets paid for it. Yes, he looks like a blue collar worker and just one of the guys, but that is his shtick and a scam to get people to believe him. Like Nietzsche, Descartes, Kant and other influential pseudo Intellectuals, Moore fails (or refuses) to see the flaw in his thinking. Shame on him! But if we accept the lies and allow the deception, it is truly *shame on us*.

I have read and truly enjoyed Bernard Goldberg's books "Bias", "Arrogance", and "100 people screwing up America". Mr. Goldberg points out the bias and the out and out lies of the media, as well as the left wing propaganda spewed out in print and on the radio and

TV from the Leftist Superstars of Hollywood. "Kids" may "say the darnedest things", but grownups say the damnedest things. Bernie sees it as mostly the fault of those doing the spewing, but isn't it really as much the fault of those who give credence to such falsehood. And, yes, there is right wing bias as well, just not as heavily entrenched as the left.

Here is the point of this chapter, it really does not matter what you believe, or how strongly you believe it, truth rules. It cannot be coerced, threatened, changed, bribed, manipulated, or otherwise made ineffective.

The Truth, about Truth is that it just is. It is our job to uncover the biases and misconceptions while preserving that, which has the evidence of being truly dependable, even if it means giving up a our own perception of what we hoped the truth to be.

Personal responsibility is the backbone of any civilization that aspires to be great. In the "sixties" most of us saw a society livid with hypocrisy, and we wanted to change things for the better. In our attempt to do so however, we adopted the techniques of the hypocrites, and instead of starting with "the truth, the whole truth, and nothing but the truth", we accepted and spewed lies just to make a point, and ended up being our father's sons.

The civil rights movement of the 60's and 70's was a most worthy cause and a lot of good people, white and black, got on the bandwagon, but so did some bad people, both white and black who saw it as a way to further a clandestine agenda.

We now have laws that protect segments of our society from unjust treatment by the populace in general. But in reality the only thing that has changed is the degree and spectrum of abuse. The law which cannot change the heart is meant to punish the one who breaks it. If he or she saw value in the law, they would not have broken it in the first place. To see value in the law requires a change of heart. Hate has a new target today, the so called intolerable Christian who thinks God's Truth still matters.

There are those who see more evil in a good and honest man with a gun in his hand, than a ruthless liar, womanizer, and cheater with a bible in his hand sitting in the oval office. Perceptions are always influenced by the value we attribute to them, which means if our value system is faulty; our perception of truth will be faulty as well. A value system that does not put truth above *everything else* will have very little lasting value.

A law that says a woman has the "right to choose" only punishes those who would refuse her the right to choose. It neither condones, nor condemns her choice regardless of what she chooses to do. The same is true of a law which ensures freedom of speech and does not condone, or condemn what the speaker has to say. Likewise' a law, which give us the right to bear arms neither condones nor condemns what that person does with a gun. Laws of freedom simply give us certain liberties to choose, but they never imply or guarantee that the person will make the right choice.

The founding fathers never intended freedoms to be viewed as an unrestricted right to do whatever we wanted. That is neither the intent nor the spirit of these types of laws. Plain common sense would tell us this. That is why so many of our founding fathers pointed out that a moral code was necessary to restrict these freedoms and protect us from those who would abuse them.

There is no law, which stipulates that a woman has the right to choose what happens to her as a result of an unwanted pregnancy. There was only the Supreme Court's decision, which viewed this as a viable interpretation of already existing laws. And why not, that is exactly what the Supreme Court was created for, to interpret law. However, there are already laws on the books that make it illegal to kill another human being. The Supreme Court does not have a right to ignore laws already on the books. What the Supreme Court has done, and it clearly was not an interpretation of law, was to decide that a fetus is not a human being. Had they used the law as their premise they would have looked at laws that stipulate that if a fetus is aborted as a result of intentional or unintentional force, the responsible person can be charged with manslaughter, either voluntary or involuntary, whichever is appropriate. The Supreme Court was not created to make laws, or to ignore laws already on the books. Just interpret laws using the Constitution as a guide line. Judges can strike down laws that they deem as unconstitutional, but with Roe v Wade they ignored the law completely. Now that Roe v Wade has been overturned, state judges need to do their part to uphold the constitutional right to life.

These are judges who have sworn an oath to uphold the Constitution of the United States, and not to change it or make it more palatable to the likings of a certain segment. In fact, the Supreme Court has a duty to make sure it does not change the law and stay within the spirit of the law as well as the letter of the law. The oath was to uphold the law, the job is to interpret with integrity, and anything else is at best, dereliction of duty and at worst, treason. Hear this Supreme Court Justices, there is a court much more supreme than you, and you will stand before this court, stripped of your robes, to answer for the judgements you hand down.

The Lord said, "Judge not, that you be not judged" Matthew 7:1 and you will be judged.

Abortion rights activists, who hate to be called Abortion Rights Activists, prefer the handle Freedom of Choice Activists because it sounds a lot nobler. They make it sound like a worthy cause, instead of the actual fundamentally base and selfish tirades that they are. They are real phonies because Abortion Rights Activists could care less about a woman's right to choose. Here's the proof: Go into a Planned Parenthood establishment (the mother of all Abortion Rights Activists) and tell them you would like an abortion but you can't afford it. They will bend over backwards to help and even pay for it. But tell them you want to keep your baby but you need help financially, they will show you the door and give you attitude to boot.

They will tell you that there are other organizations that might be able to help you, but that is not their forte, and they won't give you a list of places that might help you. So the name itself is a lie, *(i.e. Planned Parenthood* instead of *Planned Abortion)*, and their seeming concern for unwed mothers is a farce and a lie as well. Otherwise they would be willing to help with either choice, so what are they really about? Not truth!

What is their real value system saying in the light of their actions? You can know a tree by its fruit, so what fruit are they really producing. We don't care about you, we only care about our agenda which we feel will better serve humanity because we are a lot smarter and infinitely wiser than anyone who disagrees with our enlightened

philosophy. A philosophy I might add that is totally self-serving.

Let's come together and think this through. If you fight to make abortion legal, and then you offer help to the poor and down trodden to obtain an abortion, but refuse to help the same populace with child bearing and rearing, either with encouragement or financial support, the only conclusion to be drawn is that you are not trying to help that segment but eliminate it, or substantially lower that particular populace (i.e. genocide).

Genocide, the offense of killing or conspiring to kill a segment of society because of their ethnic, racial, economic, national, or religious characteristics with the final goal of exterminating the entire segment.

These are elitists, not humanitarians. They are wolves in sheep's clothing. They are supremacists of the vilest kind, who preys on the helplessness of society's weakest segment to promote an agenda of hate. They pass themselves off as humanitarians and get good people to join their cause by making them think they are helping people, when in reality they are helping lead the innocent to the slaughter. True, they never turn down anyone who wants an abortion regardless of race, ethnicity, social status, or religion, but how many Ivy League elitists do you suppose go to Planned Parenthood for help. It's not too late to stop the slaughter of innocent lives around the world.

Recently a new report came out showing that the black population in the United States has declined to third place behind Latinos. Make of that what you will, but I think these results are very revealing. Just a few years ago they predicted that the black population in the U.S. would soon catch up to, and maybe even replace the white population as the dominating majority. What happened? It does not take a rocket scientist to figure out that the black population in the United States is being systematically eliminated through disguised genocide in the form of "freedom of choice."

This was by design as Planned Parenthood was started by the racist Margret Sanger. Now many will argue about this, but all you need to do to verify this is to read her writings where she talks about eliminating the undesirables. She did not have to say blacks as it was implied in the vernacular of the day.

I have talked to many people who think that they have a right to say: "this is my truth" as if calling it their truth somehow makes it right for them. And if I have a different view of the truth, then I should keep it to myself. Well it stands to reason that if two people disagree on what the truth is, then at least one of them is wrong, and possibly both. Truth is exclusive and lies are inexhaustible. Academia has pushed numerous false doctrines down our throats to make it sound as if it is written in stone. In fact it is an over active imagination searching for excuses to promote a Woke agenda. First rule of marketing is to find what people want and that's what you sell them. And if they don't want what you're selling, you simply make them feel guilty or stupid for not seeing it your way. They are selling to your emotions and not to your sense of reasoning.

Truth is not illusive, it wants to be found. But like a fair maiden, or a prince in shining armor it wants to be loved without any outside interferences. True love does not want someone for what they could be, but for who they really are. Truth is no different, it wants to be loved for what it is. Truth is at the heart of every matter, and the heart "is" the very thing that keeps us from it. We need a change of heart, and that won't happen until we see the value of having a changed heart. Truth will not change for us, we need to change in order to fully appreciate what it has to offer.

The best definition of truth that I have ever heard came from a saying during the Viet Nam era and it gets right to the Heart of the Matter.

"It is what it is." Ignoring it will not make it go away.

Chapter 2

The Truth about Knowledge, Wisdom and Reason

In a previous chapter we discussed how know-ledge is acquired. We discussed both Empiricism and Rationalism and we discovered that the likelihood of acquiring knowledge through rational thought was insignificant at best. Know-ledge must come from previous experience that, when reasoned out, leads to a rational and logical path in the search for more experiences that will lead to more truth and knowledge.

We used Thomas Edison's invention of the light bulb as an example of knowledge through experience (or experimentation if you will). The fact is that Mr. Edison had over 1000 different patented inventions accredited to him by the time of his death. Each invention started with previous knowledge that led to experimentation that led to new knowledge. All knowledge is gained through experience. In truth, there has never been an invention based on anything outside the realm of experience. Even the computer and all the computer programs ever made have come from previous knowledge and experimentation. It could be said that the fruit of knowledge, once it is planted, and nourished, begets more knowledge. Knowledge however, is not truth in and of itself, it is only our limited understanding of truth.

Intelligence refers to the versatile efficiency of an individual's rational processes, particularly his or her comprehension, conceptualization, learning, recall, thinking and reasoning capacities. Thus intelligence is a measure of a person's capacity and effectiveness in the learning process. A person may be very intelligent without the benefit of experience and thus, know very little. A person might know thousands of facts and not have a clue or the intelligence to know what to do with them.

Intelligence however, never acts alone. Motivation to know more is critical in finding truth. There are people who have high intelligence and an overabundance of knowledge who are complacent in finding new knowledge. They are satisfied with what their experience and education has taught them because it serves *their* purpose. Thus, intelligence and knowledge equal mediocrity due to lack of motivation. What a pitiful shame.

Knowledge is meant to be used, not just acquired. Intelligence is an effective tool to acquire knowledge but if that knowledge is not used to acquire more knowledge, the cycle is broken and stagnation sets in. Truth and knowledge work hand in hand to lead us to more truth and more knowledge and to teach us the practical applications of the knowledge we have. There are however, different types of knowledge.

Factual (empirical) knowledge is simply the compilation of facts. This type of knowledge is what is taught in school (i.e. learning from others who have already experienced such knowledge either from personal or learned experiences). This knowledge would include any knowledge that could be completely transferred from one individual to another.

There is, however, knowledge that is very difficult to transmit to others, since that knowledge is something only that person has experienced, he or she is the only one who can make a proper correlation to that knowledge and its effect on that individual. This knowledge is known as tacit knowledge or expert knowledge, (i.e. by virtue of the fact that the individual is the only one to have experienced it, making that person an expert on that particular knowledge). This type of knowledge is very difficult to express unless the person who is receiving the knowledge has had the exact same experience. Personal relationships, moral upbringing, ethics or codes of conduct, all fall into this category as well as knowledge associated with procedural techniques that are as individual as a person's fingerprint. In some cases, only the person who has such knowledge sees the value of having that knowledge.

When going up or down a flight of stairs I hold on to the rail when possible to assist in my navigation due to the fact that I am handicapped. A non-handicap person may not see the value in such a procedure. I was brought up with a Christian ethic, which I find has enormous value to me. Others may not have such values simply because they have not experienced any desire to acquire such an ethic. Therefore they see no real value in it, and in fact they may see it as a deficit.

Consider if you will, the differences between wisdom, knowledge and reason. Knowledge is the accumulated information that we possess. The knowledge cannot do anything until we put it into action. Example, we know for a fact that it is raining outside. That piece of knowledge can be used. For instance we may decide to go outside and take an umbrella with us, or perhaps we will choose a raincoat, or simply decide not to go outside. We might even decide to go into the rain without any protection and take our chances against the elements.

 Now not every one of these choices is a good choice, but they are choices and all of them are based on the knowledge that it is raining. So it stands to reason that knowledge is only one tool in making decisions.

Another tool would be reason. As I said before reason is what separates us from the animals, and reason would tell us that because it's raining outside something needs to be done if we intend to go outside. Reason would tell us that although a raincoat might keep our bodies dry, it would do nothing to keep our heads from getting wet. Reasoning is a great tool, as it gives us options, but how do you deal with all the options and decide which one is best. That is where wisdom comes into play. Wisdom not only takes into consideration the physical needs but also considers comfort and values. Value being the new shirt you are wearing, not wanting to ruin it. Wisdom takes into account all available truths that may have an impact on a certain situation, so that we can find the best available solution.

Decisions can lead to ideal outcomes or less than ideal outcomes, and it always depends on the information on which we based that decision. Therefore legitimate, truthful, and complete information will leads to a more positive outcome, whereas unreliable, untested, false, or incomplete information can lead to a disaster.

Some decisions are minor or even insignificant and some are life altering. Take for instance, you leave the house without your car keys. A minor inconvenience at best. You simply go back and get them. However, if your house keys are on the same key ring, it could make for a very bad day. Having to find a phone and the number to a locksmith, waiting for the locksmith to get there and unlock the door, costing money you may not have and making you late for a very important appointment. It only took a fleeting second to cause what could be a disaster. Luckily after a few days, it is not such a big of a deal.

Now what if you forget to check the oil in your car, before you take off on a long trip? This can be a life altering deal that could leave you stranded in the middle of nowhere with a fortune in tow bills and repair bills and even motel bills all because you did not put $5 worth of oil in your car. This little, but life altering decision will stick with you for a very long time. It will likely take a month or more to recover from this bad decision.

Then there is the really bad decision to adjust the car radio while traveling at high speed on an unfamiliar road. You miss the curve and your car goes into the lane with oncoming traffic, you swerve and miss the first car that loses control and flips, but you hit the second car with five high school kids on their way to the prom. Their car explodes and your car is thrown into the ditch after it rolled what seemed to be 10 times. All in all, your little mistake has cost lives, thousands upon thousands of dollars in damages, and untold agony to a lot of families. You will never get over this bad decision.

In each one of these cases the people knew beforehand what the potential outcome of their actions could be. The knowledge was there, they simply did not apply reason and wisdom to that knowledge. Academia teaches knowledge, and knowledge is good, but if you fail to use reason and wisdom with that knowledge then knowledge is just a dusty book on a shelf, it means nothing.

One of the dumbest sayings of the modern era is that "Knowledge is Power". The fact is knowledge is only a small piece of information and does not get its power from just being a fact. The power comes when knowledge is combined with reason and wisdom. If you simply use knowledge as a tool to get what you want, you are using it under false pretenses. If you are testifying in a court of law and you intentionally mislead the court by leaving out certain details so that the outcome of the trial is advantageous to you or someone you care about, you have perverted justice. In this case knowledge was combined with greed and intentional deception, while wisdom and reason were left out. You might say then that deception has power, and to an extent it does. It has the power to fool the ignorant. Once the truth comes out the deception has lost all credibility and the perpetrator has become a perjurer in the eyes of the court. Thus truth has the true power.

Truth cannot be a subjective concept. It either is, or is not true. If true, then only the ramifications of such truth can be subjective, but only to the point of crossing another truth.

Example 1: It is cloudy outside. Ramification: I could get wet if it starts to rain.

Example 2: It is cloudy outside and it is raining. Ramification: I will get wet. The only subjective feature is in how we apply the truth. Truth does not need to be interpreted it is either a fact or it is not.

Reasoning and wisdom will teach us how to properly apply the truth to any given scenario. If the reasoning or wisdom is faulty, we will end up with a bad decision resulting in a bad outcome. The truth did not change the outcome, rather how we applied the truth with the proper or improper knowledge, reasoning and wisdom has altered the outcome.

Kierkegaard, a philosopher and existentialist, maintained that subjective truth is based in evidence and you could presume a thing to be real if that evidence was sufficient for your thesis. In other words if there is enough evidence in favor of a thesis, and no evidence to dispute it, we may assume it is truthful. Let's try two scenarios and see how this works.

Scenarios 1: Thesis: There is a God. Evidence, the universe is too organized for a happenstance. The existence of life is totally unexplainable let alone intelligent life. DNA is so unique and complicated it could not have developed by happenstance. Every organ in the body was made specifically for its intended use and placed in the body in such a particular way that the more vital organs, receive more protection from the skeleton and muscular parts of the body. Prophecy in the Bible has been proven true with astonishingly incalculable odds. I could go on forever with this proof because literally everything in this universe points to a Creation God.

For those who claim there is no evidence of God, they are either blind or ignorant of the facts.

Scenarios 2: Thesis: There are Quarks (Material inside protons and neutrons). No one has ever seen a quark but the evidence that we do have is strongly in favor of their existence. Stanford Linear Accelerator Center (SLAC) shot high-energy electrons into protons and neutrons, the reactions strongly indicated that the protons and neutrons were made up of smaller point like particles. Literally every scientist on the planet will concur that quarks exist, and there is much less evidence for quarks than there is for God's Creation and its origin. Both are truly subjective truths in that we must rely on evidence to come to an intelligent conclusion. However: the term "subjective" has been adulterated by academia to mean it's your exact truth, subject to your own bias interpretation.

Remember the prophets in Jeremiah's time that prophesied that Israel would have peace. That was an out and out lie that they spewed on those with itchy ears as if it were the word of God. They wanted and hoped it to be true. They may have even prayed for it to be true. The fact is that even when everyone believed it to be true, it was not. Had those in Jerusalem looked at the evidence: Famine, pestilence, armies surrounding the city, they would have known that the prophets were lying.

Wishing something to be true has never made it true. Wishing you were born a girl instead of a boy will never change the fact that you are a boy. Surgery after surgery will not change it either. Counseling people to change who or what they are will only change the outside appearance and maybe how they are perceived by the outside world. Inside they are still the boy and the only way to make them feel whole is council them to accept who they really are. Instead of changing the outside with surgery, they really need to change the inside to match the outside. Thus the outside will match the inside and the person will be complete and whole. Anything else is simply a placebo.

Knowledge tells us that an XY chromosome is male, wisdom tells us that we cannot change to an XX Chromosome, and reason tells us that we must accept the things we cannot change.

When we are born, there are certain traits that come with the package. Sex, eye color, hair color etc. however, our proclivities are left blank to be filled in by us. Once we reach a certain age, those proclivities we have acquired will influence our decision making. Keep in mind that we ourselves choose these proclivities, by being influenced by our surroundings, our knowledge, our wisdom and our reasoning all play a part in what we accept. In other words two people in the same environment could end up with many different proclivities due to their knowledge, wisdom and reason and their willingness to accept their preferences rather than to deal with reality as it is.

People change their hair color and even change the appearance of their eyes, but these proclivities do not change who a person is. They keep their identity. They are, after all, the very same person, but for vanities sake have changed their appearance in an attempt to become a better (in their mind) version of them-selves. This is the human condition, we are all different and we all want to be a better version of ourselves. The dilemma comes when our knowledge, wisdom and reasoning are overshadowed by our desires, ambitions, and appetites.

Don't get me wrong, desires, ambitions, and appetites can be a very good thing. They help us appreciate the things we have and help us realize the things we need. They are helpers though, and not decision makers. If it weren't for our appetite we might not eat. If it weren't for our desires we might not work and if it weren't for our ambition we might not try to do our best. But these are all motives and without the decision making of our brain, they could cause real damage. Likewise, if our Knowledge, Wisdom and Reason are governed by an untruth, our decision making will be faulty.

Some people have proclivities that influence them to act in an uncaring manner toward their neighbor. Bigotry is a perfect example of a proclivity that has developed through lifelong influences. The only people who think Bigotry is ok are the bigots. That is because at some point in their lives they accepted bigotry as part of their character. Bigotry is based on the lie which says the bigot thinks they are better than you. Telling the truth, in and of itself, is not bigotry.

Let's say that a person comes to your door collecting donations for a Gay Pride event and you say "I do not support nor can I contribute to your cause, I believe that lifestyle to be morally wrong." This is not bigotry. It is simply a person exercising their right to express themselves as their character dictates. This is the subjective truth Kierkegaard was talking about. Not just that you believe something to be true because you want it to be true, but rather you have adequate evidence that something is true and thus, you must act accordingly. Too many people think that desire equals evidence. Wanting something to be true, will never make it true. The person who bullies a young boy or girl because they are weak or different or a slow learner is truly a bigot and reflects their bad character.

Acceptance of such behavior is wrong, just like telling a gay person they are going to hell is wrong. You see, we are not their judge so we don't really know what is in their heart. God knows and therefore He is their judge. What we can say is that people who do such things are in jeopardy of judgement from God, but if we put our trust in Jesus we can accept the gift he has offered us of Salvation. You don't give up your sin to earn salvation, you admit your sin and accept salvation, and God will do the rest.

 He will plant truth and love in your heart and cause you to grow as a child of God. When you plant a tree, it takes years to see the fruit, but when you plant the right seed you know what it will look like when it is all grown up. Be patient with yourselves, if you truly are a child of God, for even Satan cannot snatch you from Gods hand. I say if, because there are too many people who claim to be children of the King, but in reality they are children of Satan. These are usually the ones who act self-righteous when you question their faith. The true Christian has nothing to be self-righteous about, they know they are sinners, and they know that "but for the Grace of God there go I".

Now the person, who assumes that they have a right to condemn another, has assumed they, themselves to be God, this is blaspheming the Creator of all that is Good, while they themselves are sinners. And for those Christians who quote a bible verse that we will judge the nations need to understand, that judgement is future tense and not meant for the present age. We do as Christians have an obligation to judge those who say that they are Christians, so if your pastor or minister says that God loves the homosexual this is a true statement, but if he says God is accepting of the homosexual lifestyle he is preaching a falsehood.

God's love and compassion is extended to all, this does not in any way affirm the actions of anyone. A parent may continue clothing and feeding a dis-obedient child even if that child has disappointed them. We love our Children and God loves his creation. But God is so much more than love; He is also Truthful and Righteous, Merciful and Just. He cannot condone anything contrary to His nature. But He gives us every chance to repent and conform to His righteousness.

The real question is not if God loves you, the real question is do you love God? And if so, do you love His Word? You cannot Love God, and hate His Word. His Word is the very character of God.

Too many times people are taking part of a truth and mixing it with a lie to come up with what they want to be the truth. A partial lie makes the whole statement a lie. Accepting a lie as the truth, knowing that there is a lie in the midst of a conclusion, is the same as telling the lie in the first place. The most egregious lies are the lies we tell ourselves. And some of the vilest lies are spewed from a pulpit or a podium.

The bible says, *"The heart is deceitful above all things, and desperately wicked: who can know it?"* Jeremiah 17:9. Now in truth the heart just pumps our blood, but common sense would tell us that it is not our actual heart to which it is referring to here. Rather it is referring to our wants and desires, which are those things that motivate us in our daily lives. Love of money may motivate us to work really hard so that we can bring home more money. It might also motivate us to steal money or cheat someone.

When we let our heart rule us, we justify in our mind that wrong is right. Thus, we deceive ourselves. Now if we deceive ourselves, who is to blame? We are, plain and simple. God gave us a brain to discern the path we should take, and he gave us a heart to motivate us on that path. The mind chooses the path and the heart motivates us on that path. When your mind allows your heart to choose the path you become lost. In order for us to feel comfortable along this wrong path we will justify our actions in our own mind.

It could be as simple as I wanted it, or you could get creative and tell yourself you were born that way. After a very short time you may actually start to believe it. That is, you have faith in a lie. This is not the faith that saves.

God wants us to put our faith in His Word. Now you can't put faith in anything or anyone until you know into whom or what you are putting your faith. Here is the problem, if you put your faith in a lie you will reap the consequences. I might believe I can fly but if I leap off of a ten story building, I will die. God is not looking for blind faith. If you went to church and prayed the sinner's prayer: that little exercise did not save you. Believing that there is a God will not save you, nor will believing in the 10 Commandments save you. Jesus said if you know Me you will know the Father. Knowing God; not just His Bible, but actually knowing Him as you would a friend, is the only way you will have the truth and thus, the faith that saves.

God gave us a free will. The fact is faith would be unattainable without free will. Loving God has to be a choice we make freely. God does not want robots. When God created man, He said *"it is good, it is very good"* Genesis 1:31. Which means God did not make any mistakes when he created you. People make the mistakes, and some people want to pin that on God. People choose who they want to be, we have always had freedom of choice. God allows us to choose to be a hero or a murderer, it's up to us. Laws are there to help us stay on the path that leads to life. The Law itself will not save you, but without it how would we know good and evil. The fruit that comes from the Knowledge of Good and Evil are the consequences of our actions. And the universal consequence is death. God could have made the best androids with all kinds of super powers. Instead He made us because androids cannot love, they can define love and even analyze love, but they cannot do it.

You might ask what love has to do with it, well I'll tell you. God created us in His Own image and after His Own likeness. He created something He could love and something that could love Him back. That is why we are children of God.

Here is our problem though, we sinned and now we have a corrupt heart. *"The heart is deceitful above all things, and desperately wicked: who can know it?* "Jeramiah 17:9. As such we are in desperate need of a savior. And Praise the Lord, He sent us one. Please understand that unless you are perfect you will have a shelf life. So God sent His Perfect Son to take our place in death so that we might recognize the perfection that is Jesus Christ and live. We don't ourselves become perfect by any means, but believing in the perfection of Jesus Christ, we through faith will be made perfect in the world to come.

For those of you who claim that LGTBQ is not covered in the New Testament, these are the verses that cover the matter.

"Likewise also the men, leaving the natural use of the woman, burned in their lust for one another, men with men committing what is shameful, and receiving in themselves the penalty of their error which was due. And even as they did not like to retain God in their knowledge, God gave them over to a debased mind, to do those things which are not fitting; being filled with all unrighteousness, sexual immorality, wickedness, covetousness, maliciousness; full of envy, murder, strife, deceit, evil-mindedness; they are whisperers, backbiters, haters of God, violent, proud, boasters, inventors of evil, disobedient to parents, undiscerning, untrustworthy, unloving, unforgiving, unmerciful; who, knowing the righteous judgment of God, that those who practice such things are deserving of death, not only do the same but also approve of those who practice them." Romans 1:27-32

Now any person with an intelligent mind can see that the world is getting more corrupt by the minute. Satan knows his time is limited and he is hard at work trying to get as many souls as possible. A corrupt world is in fact a doomed world and it will continue on a path of destruction to the very end. There is no stopping it. So you can accept the inevitable and go down with the ship, or you can grab the lifeline God has thrown out to you. It's your choice.

Chapter 3

The Truth about God

Talk about a mystery, for thousands upon thousands of years people have been praying to one god or another. Though they were convinced that their prayers would be answered they really did not know what, or who, or how a god was able to deliver on their requests. Currently there are about 10,000 different religious sects in the world. However, most are one of these four – Christianity (31%), Islam (24%), Hinduism (15%), and Buddhism (7%). Judaism is only 0.2%. Christianity Judaism and Islam = 55.2% of the world population all claiming to worship the same God.

However, Islam has a different name for their god (Allah), other than the one given by Christians and

Jews (Yahweh). Islam was not even a thing for almost 600 years after the Bible was completed, questioning whether it be man-made, and as such must exclude itself from our list. Muhammad claimed to be a Prophet. Here is the problem with that, the God of the Bible said that the time of prophecy ended with John the Baptist so according to God Himself; Muhammad could not have been a prophet, nor could Joseph Smith for that matter. *"The law and the prophets were until John: from that time the gospel of the kingdom of God is preached, and every man enters with difficulty into it"* Luke 16-16. After Jesus, there was no more need of prophets since *"Jesus had come to fulfill all the Law and the Prophets"* (not my words, His) Matthew 5:17. After Jesus there was no more need of a new law or another prophet.

So that leaves Christians and Jews as followers of the God of Abraham. Christians and Jews believe in the 39 Books of the Old Testament so basically the Jews are just 27 books shy of being Christian. Now Jesus as the Messiah replaced the Levitical priesthood with a new order as promised by God *"The LORD has sworn and will not change his mind: 'You are a priest forever, in the order of Melchizedek'"* Psalms 110:4. The Jewish Priests and elders were being threatened with losing their luster as it were and so rejected the Messiah. They continue to reject Him for the very same reason, even though they know that the entirety of the Old Testament points directly to Jesus being the Messiah. You see the Jewish people think of the Messiah as a military leader; someone who will Make Israel a Great Nation. What Israel fails to realize is that it is faith in God Himself that makes Israel a great nation.

In Christianity there are so many different faiths that it is very difficult to sort out. There is only one faith that leads us to salvation, and that is Jesus Christ who died for our sins, and has risen.

It's such a simple concept as it has been preached for 2000 years, and yet religion itself has complicated it to the extent that there are around 45,000 denominations globally, each with its own little twist. The Good News is that you do not need to belong to any *denomination* to be saved. Although the Catholics might disagree, their history alone should convince a thinking person that God is not about an elaborate ceremony, but rather obedience to His Word. Consider the confessional; the bible states plainly that only God can forgive sins. The Catholic Church wants you to believe that the priest is

God's representative hear on earth. The fact is that God had already sent His representative to earth to die for our sins; he paid it all with the cross. We don't need any more forgiveness, *"It is finished"* John 19:30.

The Catholic Church uses this ploy to keep you coming back. The Bible does say *"who's sin' you forgive they will be forgiven and who's sins you retain they will be retained"* John 20:32. Christ was talking to all Christians paraphrasing his earlier statement that God *"forgive us our sins as we forgive others"* Luke 11:4. If you still think that the priest can forgive your sins, you will die in your sins.

The only thing that is required is that you believe in one God who is the source and giver of all good, and that He sent His only Son Jesus Christ to teach us what good is and to die for us. *"For the wages of sin is death, but the gift of God is eternal life through Jesus Christ our Lord"* Romans 6:23.

There are, regrettably, many pastors and preachers who will say that what I say is my own opinion and not based in fact. The reason they say this, is because it does not fit their narrative. Everything I say in this discourse can be backed up by the Word of God itself.

Fellowship with other Christians is a wonderful experience and you can get that in any Bible preaching congregation, which is highly recommended. Non-denominational bible preaching churches are easy to find. Most have a website where you can go to find their statement of faith which states that the bible is the definitive Word of God. If that church does not believe that the whole Bible is the divinely inspired Word of God, you're in the wrong church.

James 1:27 says: 'pure and undefiled religion before God and the Father is this: to visit orphans and widows in their trouble, *and* to keep oneself unspotted from the world.'

So how do we keep ourselves unspotted? By believing and following the Word of God to the letter? Even as Christians we will still sin, the difference is we recognize our behavior as sinful and we truly want to stop sinning. That is to say, we strive to attain that character that emulates Our Lord and Savior Jesus Christ. Every true Christian knows that we can never attain the true character of Christ: not in this lifetime anyway, but by trying and persisting to attain that character we perfect our faith.

If we believe and confirm that what God says in His Word, that that which is evil is in fact sin, whether we are able to comply 100% of the time or not, we are keeping ourselves free from the world view. So many religions including Catholics are capitulating to their congregations in order to maintain member-ship. God is not interested in membership He is looking for true believers. If a pastor or preacher or even a lay person fails to tell you that your sin is wrong, how will you know to repent. If that same pastor, preacher or lay person fails to tell you about the grace that God gives the sinner, why would you want to repent?

So who is this God that wants us to follow His rules and believe He will do what He says He will. We need to go back to the creation of everything to find the answer. First God created the Heavens and the Earth on day one, and after-wards he said it was good. After every day of creation God said it was good, and finally on the last day God said it was very good. Here is the truth, all good comes from God. If you say "I was the one who helped the old lady cross the street" The most you can say is that by the grace of God I was able to help the lady. Likewise; nothing that is evil comes from God.

A lot of people have said the God of the Bible is too judgmental. But Jesus said *"And if any man hears my words, and believes not, I judge him not: for I came not to judge the world, but to save the world"* John

12:47. If Jesus had come to judge the world we would all be guilty and deserving of death. If you are looking for a culprit, Satan is the accuser. He indeed says you are guilty, but Jesus says to Satan, "Back off, this one is mine."

A judge (no matter his rank) who does not judge according to both man's law and God's Law, for all judges swear or affirm to God Himself and as such will be judged by God for those judgements. And if you judged wrongly and do not repent you are in danger of spending an eternity separated from God, not just for your sins but for the sins of those who were set free from your judgement. Likewise the pastors, preachers and teachers who teach that sin is ok, you will pay for your sins as well as the sins of those you have misled. Having all the sins, of all these people that were led astray, on their head: now that is a scary scenario. And even what I do here, if I lead anyone into sin, their sin will be on my head, but likewise if God indeed taught me these things and I failed to show them to you, I would be guilty of sin and your sin would be on my head.

Consider this, before God said let there be light there was only darkness. Darkness is not something, but rather the absence of something. Likewise: evil is not something, but rather the absence of good. We have all heard the term "he or she is no good" to describe a person. But have you ever heard the term "he or she is no evil", of course not, with the possible exception when referring to Jesus who had *no* evil in Him.

This world is full of evil and keeps getting worse. The simple fact is that there is a severe lack of good in our society. And many who think they are doing good are only fooling themselves. Mega churches are just one example of people who think they are doing Gods will by supporting the "feel good lie". God does want you to be prosperous, but in His Word, which is the true wealth. Those who attend the prosperity gospel churches are worshiping money and not God.

There have been many people who said that God is evil because he killed 180,000 men from Sennacherib; however, God only sent His angel to pull the good (that rightfully belongs to Him) from the Assyrians. When all the good has been taken away evil will do its ungodly work, and men will turn on each other. He is after all God, and we are His creation, so

He gets to call the shots. There is nothing evil about God reclaiming the good which is rightfully His.

Which brings us to the question: why did God create man in the first place? Let's look at the circumstances of man in the garden. Man was placed in the garden surrounded by trees that were *good* for man to consume. Let's call these the trees of virtues. Now there was the tree of Life in the center of the garden (which is perfection), we will call that the perfect character (i.e. Jesus), and also the Tree of the knowledge of Good and Evil (choice). God created us that we might consume of the trees of virtue and build our character to the point of perfection thus consuming the Tree of Life and live forever as children of God. Now perfect good was God's plan for us, but without a choice we would have been as it were slaves to good, and God did not want slaves but rather free men. And free men are free to choose good or evil. God created us that we might share in His Goodness, not just receiving God's goodness, but also sharing it with others. Thus we become children of God.

Many are confused about the practice of communion. Jesus at the Last Super gave us this command. When we eat the bread we taste the perfect goodness and character of Jesus. And when we drink the cup, we taste the full and total commitment that Jesus has to His character. Now the life is in the blood that Jesus shed, and the blood represents Jesus's Commitment to the Word of God. So if we are covered in the blood, we need to be totally committed to the Word also. And that is what Satan hates, that we have a choice we can make, to get out of Satan's Control. If we are only committed to the parts of the Word that we like, we are not covered in the blood and in jeopardy of losing our salvation to the world view.

You see Satan thought he pulled one over on God, but in fact it was God's plan from the beginning to give us choice. There seems to be a great schism in churches today regarding Calvinism vs Arminianism. Consider this if you will, we know that God is a just God and if God choose those who were to be saved and not offered salvation to all, that would not be just. Thus simply by knowing the character of God, we know that Calvinism is on shaky ground. Here is the good news, if you truly believe that Jesus Christ is the son of God, and you believe that God is a just God, and you repent of your sins, you are saved. But if you think that God could be unjust you are dead in your sin, and in fact you have blasphemed the Spirit of God.

Saying God is unjust, unloving, untruthful, unmerciful, unwise, unknowing or unholy is blaspheming the Spirit and Unforgivable in this world and the next.

So *who is this Satan*? Well I'll tell you. What is the opposite of eternity? You might think it is death, but the opposite of death is life. The opposite of eternity is time. And time is without question the ruler of this world. Time affects absolutely everything physical in the universe and unless it is perfect, it has a shelf life.

Even Jesus when he came was subject to time, knowing that he had a finite amount of time to accomplish His mission here on earth. Even though He was subject to time in a physical body, His spirit and his character were not, thus His physical body died, but His Spiritual Body, being perfected, rose from the dead. Satan in the garden had no power over Adam and Eve while they were in the garden, so the snake tempted Eve so that Man through the fall would be subject to him.

Keeping in mind that we are created in the image and after the likeness of God, we must consider what this means. God is all knowing, we have the ability to know, but our knowing is extremely limited. God also has a Spirit. We know that Love and Truth are Spirits of God. What are love and truth? Love motivates action and truth motivates, well everything. That is why it says in the Bible that the Spirit of Truth proceeds from the Father. Truth motivates everything our Father in Heaven does. Thus the Father is God's Authority (i.e. the person that makes the decisions) and the Spirit of God's (is the person that Motivates Gods decisions). That explains two out of the three persons in the Godhead. The third person of the Trinity, the Son well let's look at it as a family. My dad made all the decisions when I was growing up. But my Mom motivated my Dad on what decision's to make. When I was growing up I wanted to be like my dad and mom so I tried to act like them whenever I was doing my chores. In other words I tried to emulate my parents (i.e. put on their character). God the Father is the authority (by virtue of His Dominance). The Spirit is the motivator (i.e. Helper). And the Son is the very Character, or Word of God.

We all have three persons in our one being, we have a brain to make decisions with, we have a spirit to motivate us, and then there is our character that does all the work. If we only listened to our brain we might choose anger instead of love. If we only listened to our motives we might choose to have fun and never get any work done. Our choices and actions reflect our character. With God all three are one.

Using the Word of God as a *focal* point, consider this. Jesus said that we should be perfect even as our Father in Heaven is perfect. Now we know that Jesus Himself was perfect so why did He say *"be perfect even as your Father in Heaven is perfect"* Matthew 5:48. Why didn't Jesus just use Himself as a model of perfection? If we could be perfect as Jesus is perfect we would no longer need a Savior. So we need to put on the character of Jesus to the best of our ability, but we will fail to be perfect, we are after all human and still living in a world controlled by Satan.

How then are we to be perfect? We can know the Father and His Authority, through His Word and through His Son. We can know these things perfectly, but not from books or schooling, God Himself will teach you. "Here is the rub" as they say, God will only teach you if you truly want to know Him and enter into a relationship with Him through His Word. Through faith that what God says, He will do. Through the life Jesus lived and His teaching, we can see the Father. The Father gave Jesus His Authority so that we could know the Father through the Son.

Many people have been taught to put their faith in religion. Religion will not save you; in fact religion is a hindrance to your faith. God alone is infallible, not the pope, not any man, they are human just like us. Jesus told us to call no man father (Matt 23:9) yet the Catholic Church has given the title to almost a half million priests. Yes they have excuses for everything they do. They changed the 10 Commandments for centuries. Tablets of stone written in God's own hand, my guess is that if God wrote them in stone He did not want them changed. When you change the Word of God, (and the Word became flesh) you are nailing it to the cross. And if one Pope Changed the Word of God and the others allowed it that would make the papacy an anti-Christ. There are many anti-Christs in the world today, as many as have changed the Word and have denied God. By our reasoning of the facts we have found the truth. Facts Don't Lie. Other religions are the same in that they change the meaning of God's Word for various reasons. The true religion is a relationship with God through His Word.

Now God knows good, and evil, but He always chooses good, being motivated by His Holy Spirit. How do we know this? By His Character, that came down to Earth and lived a perfect life among us. And how do we know this, because we have eye witnesses to this fact. How can we trust these eye witnesses? Because each and every one of them were willing, and in fact did, face death because of their testimony. Nobody is willing to die for what they know to be a lie. Nobody is willing to receive 40 lashes minus one for a lie. And Paul did it three times. All the Apostles suffered for their faith and yet not one recanted their story. Throughout all the Christian persecutions more than 1,000,000 have been martyred. Willingly suffering gruesome deaths rather than recanting and turning their back on the Living God.

How do we know that the Bible is true? "After many millions of man-hours of research and evidence analysis, archaeology has repeatedly confirmed the reliability of the Bible. The Bible has been proven geographically and proven over and over again historically accurate, in the most exacting detail, by external evidences." (Institute for Creation Research)[2]

For those of you who are still skeptical about the existence of God and His Book here are some facts.

---

[2] Institute for Creation Research (web page https://www.icr.org/scientific-accuracy) Scientific Accuracy(12-09-2024)

324 prophecies about Jesus have been fulfilled and many of them were in the Book of Samuel. The oldest known copy of the book of Samuel is from 200 BC two centuries prior to Jesus being born, and it is virtually word for word of those written today. So now we have absolute proof that the Bible was not changed to accommodate the New Testament. Now if only 8 of those 324 prophecies came true, (and in fact all 324 have been fulfilled, with the exception of those in Revelations) but the odds of just 8 being fulfilled is 1 with 17 zeroes behind it. So the odds of all of them coming true (which they are) would be 40 times 17 or 1 with 680 zeros behind it. That would be more than 7 times the number of atoms in the whole universe. The proof cannot be denied. When you add the fact that they all happened to only one man out of 120 billion people who have walked the earth, the number

becomes incalculable. This could only happen if indeed there is a God, and He is what He says He is. Here are 11 of the 324 verses that foretell the Messiah:

Isaiah 7:14-----Matthew 1:22 – 23 Born of a Virgin

Micah 5:2------------------Matt 2:1 Born in Bethlehem

Jeremiah 23:5-6-----Luke 1:32-33 Descended from David

Isaiah 40:3----Matt 3:1-3 Preceded by a messenger

Zechariah 9:9-----Matt 21:6-7 Ride on a donkey's colt

Zechariah 11:12-13------Matt26:14-15 30 pieces of silver

Isaiah 53:7-------Matt 27:12-14 Silent before His accusers

Psalm 22:16-----------John 20:25-27 Hands and feet pierced

Isaiah 53:12------------Mark 15:27-28 Crucified with sinners

Isaiah 53:9-----Matt 27:57-60 Buried in rich man's tomb

Psalm 16:8-10-----Acts 2:22-36 His body will not decay

All the above have eye witness accounts that they did, indeed happen.

The New Testament has 5,800 completed or fragmented Greek manuscripts, the most of any ancient writings. When these manuscripts were examined they found only cursory mistakes (i.e. letters left out or words misspelled) making it the most accurate compilation of ancient manuscripts ever found. For reference: the Iliad has 1800 manuscripts and the earliest version "Venetus A" is 1000 years old which was made over 1800 years after its supposed creation. On the other hand, Portions of the Bibles Old Testament date back to 200 BC, and the New Testament Dates to 200 AD. So they are much closer to the time period of the events.

Considering the preponderance of the evidence it would be a huge mistake not to put your faith in the Bible. But does that actually prove a creative God. Let's reason this out. For a book to be this accurate to the original manuscripts would indicate that a divine intervention might be involved. The sheer complexity of every living thing and even things that are not living must be accounted to a sort of divine intervention (i.e. a designer of indescribable and unimaginable intellect.) Every prophecy in the Bible has come true and the odds are so astronomical it must have come from a divine source. Is this proof, no but the preponderance of the evidence is enough for everyone to put faith in the God of the Bible.

This makes Bible believing Christians who accept that they are not perfect, but see and believe the perfection of Jesus Christ, the true believers God has called to be His children. No other religion on the planet can give you the peace and hope that is readily available to all who are willing to believe.

If you refuse to accept the obvious, you will have no one to blame but yourself. You see when God comes to meet the believers in the air; He will also take everything that belongs to Him i.e. *All Good*. There will be no more compassion, no more love, no more comradery, no more warmth, no more courage, no more truth and no more God. The terrors, the hate, the darkness and the utter coldness will be what are left, leaving only a misery so profound that even the most evil person could not dream it up on his worst enemy. And those who choose not to believe that Jesus Christ is the Son of God, it becomes their choice to be separated from God for all eternity.

So many people are under the impression that God is the enemy and that he is out to get them. If that were the case Jesus would have led an army to destroy all the sinners which, as it turned out is everybody. The reality is that God sent His only son to save us sinners from a fate that is much worse than death. All we have to do is: first admit we are sinners, secondly we have to believe that Jesus Christ is in fact the Son of God, and that He died for our sins and arose on the third day. All of which we have many eye witnesses who testified with their lives.

After the death of Moses, Satan and Michael fought over the body of Moses. Satan wanted to lead the

Israelites and he thought with the body of Moses he could convince Israel to follow him. As it is Satan has taken over most churches and religions around the world. If your church does not claim that Jesus is in fact one of the personages of God you are in the wrong church. If your church neglects the Old Testament which was the bible at the time of Jesus and knowing that the Old Testament is the Word of God just as much as the New Testament, you're in the wrong church. If your church makes you feel good about yourself instead of feeling good about what God has done for us, you're in the wrong church. If your pastor tells you God loves you no matter what, you have the wrong pastor. If your pastor tells you that God wants you to be rich and to prove your faith you must put your love offering in the till, you have the wrong pastor.

God Loves Truth and Justice, in fact all truth and justice comes from God, which means we must approach God on His terms not ours. God is Spirit and we need to worship Him in Spirit and Truth. We must first worship in truth, then in love and understanding and justice, not with rituals and processions.

If we don't realize we are sinners, how will we ever repent? Here is a very sad fact; those who have chosen a lifestyle contrary to the Word of God are not very likely to repent because of the public nature of their circumstances. Here is the Good News, if in fact they do repent, God will accept them with open arms. It is totally your choice to make. By the way, you will not be able to change your lifestyle simply by repenting; it will be a work- in- progress until the day you die. God knows your power is limited and so you will need to ask God for strength every day, and even then you will fail at times. But trust God, He has you completely where He wants you. Truthfully, if you don't give up on God, He will never give up on you. If we don't repent, how will we see the perfection of the Son of God? Does God love us? He loved us enough to send His only begotten Son to die on a cross for us. God's commitment to us is more than evident. God did the hard part; all we have to do is believe that He did it.

The Jews are Indeed God's chosen people. When Abraham believed God, God tested him by telling him to sacrifice his son Isaac. When Abraham proved his faith in God, God blessed all of Abraham's descendants. And God being a righteous God sent His only begotten Son to die on the cross for our sins. So then, the real children of Abraham are those who believe that Jesus is the Son of God, as Paul says, the Jew first then the gentile. So the actual descendants of Abraham have such a hope in that they are as the first born and as such inherit as a first born.

For those of you, who are reluctant to repent, let me set your mind at ease, repenting does not mean you will "sin no more". We still have the same problem we had when Adam sinned in the garden. We are still lacking the Character of God. Once we are resurrected we will have a new body and we will be resurrected into the Character of God. By faith we become children of God, and by grace we become like God.

Now the Law was written in stone. The Law will never change even though religion wants to make it more palpable. But skirting the law or ignoring the ones that they don't agree with, they lead their followers down the wrong path, and that path leads to death. Those religions that think they can change God's Word are beating against an immovable object. God will not yield to anyone. Jesus did not yield even when He knew they would hang Him on a cross.

Most Mega Churches succeed because they play on your emotions, making you feel good about yourself. It's a pleasant dream, but when you wake up it will not be so pleasant. We are all sinners and have absolutely no reason to feel good about ourselves. A true Christian knows he is a sinner, but knows that God has offered us a miraculous solution and eternal life simply by believing in His Son, our Lord and Savior, Jesus Christ.

Now we have established that Jesus Christ is indeed the character of God, and we know that the Spirit of God descended on Him at His baptism. Everything Jesus did was motivated by Gods Spirit. We also know that the Father gave Him His own authority so that He could accomplish all that the Father commanded Him. So in reality all those who saw Christ saw God Himself. We also know that Jesus was very approachable when He said: *"Let the children come to me and do not hinder them, for such is the Kingdom of Heaven"* Matthew 19:14. Thus we know that God Himself is approachable even to us sinners.

Many people refuse to come to Christ because they think that all the fun is gone, but in reality the fun is just starting. Some of the most miserable people you come across have all their physical need met and even an abundance of wealth and realize that there is something missing in their lives. In fact most people are not satisfied with their position in life. The only thing that will fill that void is *"the peace of God, which surpasses all understanding"* Philippians 4:7. When you have received this peace you will be full and complete.

The only way to know God is through His Word. Churches might preach a sermon every Sunday, usually based on one or two verses in the Bible. However: there are 31,102 verses in the Bible so a church goer might actually hear about one or two hundred verses in a year. With that in mind, for the average person to hear all of the Word of God in a church setting without any repeats would take about

1500 Sundays, or 28 years. So just going to Church on Sunday will not suffice. Jesus was willing to go to the Cross and suffer unimaginable pain, so is it too much to ask us to get to know Him by reading His Word daily?

Religious leaders twist God's Word to fit their agenda, or they change one of the commandments as the Catholic Church did, or they misuse God's Word to preach a prosperity gospel. They teach the message completely out of context such as: *"Give and it will be given to you. A good measure, pressed down, shaken together and running over, will be poured into your lap" Luke 6:38*. Here God is clearly talking about giving of ourselves. God wants us to give of our time, give assistance, give compassion, give of our possessions, and give understanding and knowledge to those who need it and will accept it. Use your God given brain; Jesus loved the apostles very much and yet not one of them achieved financial success. The false preachers who lead lost sheep to the slaughter, actually believe that God wants them to be millionaires.

God's riches and blessings are so much more than mere money, and they will never see that because they are looking in the wrong place.

What is the Seal of the Living God? Is it not faith that God is good, and that *all good comes from God*? God's Grace is a wonderful gift that all people have experienced every day. Yet it is rarely recognized for what it really is. Each day we receive a new day and a new chance to get to know the Creator of the Universe.

But God's grace will end for many in the last days. Don't waste another day in getting to know the Creator of all that is good. The seal is faith that God is who He says He is and that everything God has done in His Word and in His Actions and in His motives is always good, all the time. Believing that God is who He says He is, He give us His Spirit, that is the true seal. But if you don't know Him, how will you believe. Faith is not something you do; it is a whole new way of life, being led by the Spirit unto all Truth.

God is good, He is all good and He created us to be like him. We can be good, we can't however, be all good, nor can we be good all the time. We are trapped in a body that has no defense against evil. Once we give ourselves over to faith in Christ, we receive the Spirit of good. In other words we are motivated by the

Spirit of God to do good, and when we fail, and we will fail frequently, we recognize the sin and repent each and every time. By doing so we are showing our faith even through our failures. What a remarkable gift God has given us, the gift of faith. As we work to get closer to God through reading His Word and through prayer, Satan will be tormenting us with every kind of sin and he knows our weaknesses so that is where he will attack. If even the Angels dare not go up against Satan, how will we defeat him? We can't but we have a Savior who has already defeated him and by doing so He defeated him for us as well. And all we need to do is have faith that Jesus came from the Father and through His sacrifice on the cross, He paid the price for us, and that He rose from the dead on the third day defeating Satan and death.

When Jesus met sinners he did not make them feel condemned. What He said was, *"I am the Truth, the Way and the Life, no one comes to the father except through Me"* John 14:6-7.

We can know the father, His Goodness, His Lovingkindness, His Truth, His Authority, His Justice, His Majesty, His Eternity and His plan for us. And we can know this perfectly through Jesus Christ, even if we cannot do it ourselves.

When a person goes to the Seminary they learn about God, and those who have Doctorates know a lot about God. But none of that learning will help them to know God. It takes a personal relationship to get to know anyone. I could probably tell you an awful lot about Julius Caesar but I could not tell you if he had a sense of humor. You would have to get to know him, to know such personal details. I can with great accuracy tell you that God has an amazing sense of humor. All good comes from God including humor.

Many think to themselves "I'm not such a bad person, I give to charities, I am courteous to others, and I don't steal or break any of the major commandments so I think I will be OK when I die." If that is you, you will have a rude awakening when you die. *"For whoever keeps the whole law and yet stumbles at just one point is guilty of breaking all of it"* James 2:10. That's the same as saying if you jaywalk, you will be charged with murder, theft, adultery, blasphemy, and every other crime on the books. The reason is simple; the punishment for sin is death. You cannot avoid it unless you put your faith in Jesus, We are not perfect, but we can know perfection through Jesus. We cannot pay the price ourselves. We would have to live a perfect life completely sin free and we would have to endure the ultimate pain and suffering Jesus did without complaint.

This is such a gift; the gift itself is totally free. We will not see this gift even if it was right in front of us, unless we repent of our sins and accept Jesus as our Savior. By doing so we are simply accepting the gift. People pay thousands of dollars to take their families to Disneyland, or other more frivolous vacation locations usually lasting two weeks. This gift is free, an all-expense paid eternity at the greatest place; well anywhere.

But let's, for a minute consider the alternative. What if we reject God, and Jesus, and the whole guilty of sin thing? What's the worst that could happen to us? Most people think that they will just die and that will be the end: just nothingness. Well that philosophy does not make any sense. If those who accept God's gift are perfected by being filled with God's goodness and thus live eternally to God, then those who reject God will be completely devoid of the goodness of God, and as such are perfected in evil and thus live an eternity with absolute evil all around them. Dante in all his imagination could not come up with a more Hellish place.

All good comes from God, and as such He deserves all the praise for all good. Not us. We must take the responsibility for our sins. If we do that now we can get a full pardon, but if we wait until we are dead the pardon is off the table.

Some will say that if all good comes from God, then why are they held to the flames for not having that good? God gives good freely to all. If you saw any value in the good you would have asked for it and God would have given it gladly. If we choose evil it is entirely our choice.

You might be thinking that God can never forgive you for the things you have done. Well God's capacity for goodness and mercy is limitless, so He's got you covered. The gift is for everyone, but it does have an expiration date, so now is the time. It's as simple as this, God created us to do good, we can't be all good all the time, so God offered us a way to do good for all eternity, simply by showing us what true good is through His Son Jesus Christ.

But since we can only know true good, but not do it, this is the "Seal of the Living God". This seal is on the head (is known) and not the hands (can't do it). We, on the other hand, can choose to accept the lies that Satan wants us to believe, (the sign of the Beast), as well as living the lies, and thus the mark of the beast is on the head and the hand. So even if you do not break Gods Law, but reject it and agree with those who do break God's Law, you are as guilty as those who break the law.

We have all heard of the sin that can never be forgiven in this world and the next, that is blasphemy against the Holy Spirit found in Matt 12:32. That sin is worshiping the lie that God has evil motives. If you, having heard the truth and rejecting it, cling to the lie, you have sealed your fate with Satan. If, on the other hand you reject the lie by accepting the whole truth you will be saved. You must first accept that you are a sinner, and also accept that Jesus overcame the lie, by death on the cross, and overcame death with truth of which He is. He is The Truth, The Way and The Life. The Truth i.e. The Father, The Way i.e. The Spirit, and The Life i.e. The Son, and so is the mystery of the Trinity. Jesus, by virtue of being the character of God is the True Tree of Life.

The Truth: His authority is all good all the time. His Way: His motives are all good all the time. His Life: He does all good, all the time. There is no other good than what comes directly from God.

Now we as sinners can never defeat sin or Satan, and you might think that God has not defeated Satan either since there is still sin in the world. Remember the parable of the tares.

"Another parable He put forth unto them, saying, the kingdom of heaven is likened unto a man who sowed good seed in his field: But while men slept, his enemy came and sowed tares among the wheat, and went his way. But when the blade was sprung up, and brought forth fruit, then appeared the tares also. So the servants of the householder came and said unto him, Sir, didst not thou sow good seed in thy field? From whence then hath it tares? He said unto them, an enemy hath done this. The servants said unto him, Wilt thou then that we go and gather them up? But he said,

nay; lest while ye gather up the tares, ye root up also the wheat with them. Let both grow together until the harvest: and in the time of harvest I will say to the reapers, Gather ye together first the tares, and bind them in bundles to burn them: but gather the wheat into my barn" Matthew 13:24-30.

When Jesus comes to take the faithful out of the world, He will take all that belongs to Him as well. All Good will be taken from this world and like the Assyrians those left in the world will destroy one another. So evil will destroy itself. This is evidence based subjective truth (i.e. Faith).

People hold on to lies for many reasons. Some are trying to get back at someone who hurt them, some are trying to get ahead the easy way, some are ashamed of their lifestyle and thus do not want to come into the light. What-ever lie you are clinging to, and you really know that it is a lie in your heart, you need to let it go, God's Truth overcomes the darkness within, and His Truth will set you free.

Conclusion:

A Call to Share the Light

As the final words of this book settle in your heart, the journey does not end—it begins anew. *The Seal of the Living God* is more than a message for the few; it is a call that echoes across generations, across nations, across hearts. What you have read, what you have discovered, is meant to be shared.

In a world desperate for truth, clarity, and hope, you now carry a flame. Let it not remain hidden. Speak boldly. Share freely. Whether through a conversation, a post, a gift of this book, or simply living out its truths—your voice matters. If this message has stirred something within you, you are not alone. There are others searching for the very truths you now hold. Be the bridge. Be the spark. Help carry this message to the next soul waiting in silence.

Spread the Seal. Proclaim the truth. Let the world know: God is not silent. His seal is upon His people.

To all the people who have shared the love of Christ with me throughout my life I pray that you all know how much you have helped me and your input has definitely added to the content of this book.

Thank you for walking this path. Now, let's walk it forward—together, after all it does say *"until "**we**" put a seal on the foreheads of the servants of our God."*

Thanks

Friends for an eternity

Tom Coyle

www.ingramcontent.com/pod-product-compliance
Lightning Source LLC
Chambersburg PA
CBHW071755120626
46550CB00002B/805